Inside Job

A thriller

Brian Clemens

Samuel French — London
New York - Toronto - Hollywood

© 1993 BY CLEMENS ENTERPRISES LTD

Rights of Performance by Amateurs are controlled by Samuel French Ltd, 52 Fitzroy Street, London W1P 6JR, and they, or their authorized agents, issue licences to amateurs on payment of a fee. **It is an infringement of the Copyright to give any performance or public reading of the play before the fee has been paid and the licence issued.**

The Royalty Fee indicated below is subject to contract and subject to variation at the sole discretion of Samuel French Ltd.

> Basic fee for each and every
> performance by amateurs   Code M
> in the British Isles

The Professional Repertory Rights in this play are controlled by Samuel French Limited

The Professional Rights, other than Repertory Rights, in this play are controlled by John Redway and Associates Limited, 16 Berners Street, London W1P 3DD

The publication of this play does not imply that it is necessarily available for performance by amateurs or professionals, either in the British Isles or Overseas. Amateurs and professionals considering a production are strongly advised in their own interests to apply to the appropriate agents for consent before starting rehearsals or booking a theatre or hall.

ISBN 0 573 01792 1

Please see page iv for further copyright information

INSIDE JOB

First produced by Sally Hughes at The Mill Theatre, Sonning, on 23rd August 1988.

Suzy	Barbara Kellermann
Larry	Robin Sachs
Alex	Gary Raymond

Directed by Ted Craig
Designed by Michael Pavelka

Subsequently produced at The Theatre Royal, Windsor, on 12th April 1989.

Suzy	Prunella Gee
Larry	Robin Sachs
Alex	Gareth Thomas

Directed by Mark Piper
Designed by Julian Saxton

COPYRIGHT INFORMATION

(See also page ii)

This play is fully protected under the Copyright Laws of the British Commonwealth of Nations, the United States of America and all countries of the Berne and Universal Copyright Conventions.

All rights including Stage, Motion Picture, Radio, Television, Public Reading, and Translation into Foreign Languages, are strictly reserved.

No part of this publication may lawfully be reproduced in ANY form or by any means—photocopying, typescript, recording (including video-recording), manuscript, electronic, mechanical, or otherwise—or be transmitted or stored in a retrieval system, without prior permission.

Licences for amateur performances are issued subject to the understanding that it shall be made clear in all advertising matter that the audience will witness an amateur performance; that the names of the authors of the plays shall be included on all programmes; and that the integrity of the authors' work will be preserved.

The Royalty Fee is subject to contract and subject to variation at the sole discretion of Samuel French Ltd.

In Theatres or Halls seating Four Hundred or more the fee will be subject to negotiation.

In Territories Overseas the fee quoted above may not apply. A fee will be quoted on application to our local authorized agent, or if there is no such agent, on application to Samuel French Ltd, London.

VIDEO RECORDING OF AMATEUR PRODUCTIONS

Please note that the copyright laws governing video-recording are extremely complex and that it should not be assumed that any play may be video-recorded for whatever purpose without first obtaining the permission of the appropriate agents. The fact that a play is published by Samuel French Ltd does not indicate that video rights are available or that Samuel French Ltd controls such rights.

Other plays by Brian Clemens published by Samuel French Ltd:

Edge of Darkness
Shock!

Other plays by Brian Clemens and Dennis Spooner published by Samuel French Ltd:

Anybody for Murder?
Sting in the Tale
Will You Still Love Me in the Morning?

This play is dedicated to the memory
of my dear friend and colleague
DENNIS SPOONER (1932-1986)

CHARACTERS

Suzy
Larry
Alex

The action takes place over two days in a Spanish villa in the foothills not so very far from Marbella

AUTHOR'S NOTE

In the main text the character Suzy is described as "about 30". This, however, is not mandatory, and it would be perfectly possible for an older actress to play the role; the only criterion being that she is attractive. Nor would it be necessary to alter the text — although one could add to Suzy's last speech on page 6 to read, " ... and a good and willing body, that isn't getting any younger".

The action takes place in a Spanish villa situated in some isolation in the foothills a mile or two north of the fleshpots of the Costa del Sol.

ACT I

Scene 1

The interior of a Spanish villa situated in some isolation in the foothills a mile or two north of the fleshpots of the Costa del Sol. It is early afternoon on a pleasant, late summer's day

The main living area of an expensive and beautiful Spanish villa. It is a thoughtful conversion of an old farmhouse, retaining much of the original character; thus there are no picture windows, and such windows as there are are small and can be shuttered. One of these windows has small leaded lights of various coloured glass. A front door opens on to a terrace, with a cool and shaded area beyond. Stairs lead up to bedrooms. Close to the foot of the stairs some Toledo steel daggers are displayed. Another door leads to the kitchen area. It is open at the moment, affording us a good view into part of the area: the impression is of a pristine, gleaming white tiled kitchen

There is also a mirror, a sofa, a phone, a three-branched candelabra, an important-looking desk with chair to match, and behind the desk hangs a large oil painting. There is an open fireplace with a gas artificial log fire. Also a small table with a drinks tray and a transistor radio. When the Curtain *rises Flamenco music plays, the singer's voice a plaintive wail. The music then stops, to be replaced by a babble of chat from a Spanish announcer*

Suzy enters down the stairs. She is a strikingly attractive woman of about thirty with a superb figure that, despite its slimness, is almost voluptuous, and heightened by the elegantly sexy outfit she wears—a close fitting kind of sarong and a deeply plunging shirt blouse

Suzy crosses to switch off the radio, and the silence is profound. She looks around the area, a small air of tension about her. As she hears the sound of a car approaching she reacts, swinging round to stare at the door. For a few moments she is transfixed , but then she quickly moves to the mirror to check and primp her appearance; as an afterthought, she undoes another button on her shirt, pulls it down and wider, then opens the sarong a fraction wider, the better to reveal a long, slim leg. She wants to look sexy

We hear the car come up, stop, and then a door slam. Suzy's tension seems to increase, then, almost bracing herself, forcing a more casual air, she moves to open the door and Larry enters

Larry is in his thirties and at his prime. Handsome, with a body he takes good care of, and a terrific tan that he works at — he makes sure that you see both, with his shirt slashed down to his waist. He likes to show his even white teeth too, in a kind of semi-tough, acquired grin; Larry is a lady killer who usually gets what or who he wants. He has gold at his throat and wrists, wears white Gucci loafers and immaculately pressed slacks — he exudes a kind of arrogant confidence. Back in South London (where he comes from, and sometimes we detect it in his voice) he'd definitely be known as "Jack the Lad". He's intelligent, with a kind of animal cunning, and his speech is peppered with Americanisms. You might take him to be a pulled-up-by-his-bootlaces disc-jockey, or a high transfer-fee foot-baller

For a moment he regards Suzy, then grins, and taps his gold watch

Larry Dead on time. Or this goes straight back to Rolex.
Suzy Nobody saw you?
Larry Who's there around to see? It's pretty lonely up here ...

Suzy steps back and Larry fully enters the area to look around

Yeah, you've really got the place to yourselves. Some pad too. Nice. Very nice.
Suzy We rent it.
Larry Ve-ry nice. (*He turns to regard her*) Like you. Well, better than "nice"— terrific. (*He moves to lightly touch her blouse and the open-sided sarong*) I like this. And all for me, eh? What time will your husband be back?
Suzy Not until tonight. Late tonight.
Larry You sure about that?

Suzy I'm sure.

Larry 'Cos the last thing I want is a fracas — me and the outraged spouse. (*Grinning*) I can't afford the publicity. Now let's talk about the *first* thing I want ...

He tries to embrace her, but she pulls free

Suzy Wouldn't you like a drink?

Larry *Comme ci, comme ça...* OK, I'll join you. Can see you need one, need to loosen up, relax. But nothing heavy — a spritzer. (*He pats his stomach*) I like to stay in shape. (*He watches her as she mixes the drinks*) But you already noticed that, didn't you? Down at the Beach Club? I noticed you noticing.

Suzy How could I help noticing? The high board, the press-ups? You're not exactly an introvert!

Larry I wouldn't do it if I wasn't good at it. (*He moves close to her*) Wouldn't do nothing I wasn't good at. Nothing at all. You liked what you saw, didn't you?

Suzy You're a very attractive man, Larry.

Larry Come on! Admit it. You picked me up!

Suzy I did not!

Larry All right, all right, if it helps your pride, maybe I did look at you first — but what you were wearing — or nearly wearing — who wouldn't?

Suzy You spoke to me ...

Larry About ten seconds before *you* would have spoken to me. Anyway, what's it matter who spoke first, it was always gonna happen, wasn't it?

Suzy Yes. Inevitable.

Larry There you are then. (*He takes the drink she proffers, and swigs*) Cheers. (*Then he quickly puts the drink down and moves to embrace her*) Now, let's give the word "siesta" some meaning!

Suzy Please, Larry ... (*She pulls free from him*)

Larry What the hell's going on? The big "come on" and now nothing! I don't get it. And the way things are shaping up, I'm not going to! You some kind of tease? Is that your game ...? 'Cos listen, there's plenty more down on that beach and ——

Suzy Can't we just talk for while first?

Larry Now that's more like it. "Talk *first*." Suggests there's going to be a "second", something after the talking stops! OK. We'll talk.

He takes her hand and leads her to sit down on the sofa with him

That's better. Now what'll we talk about, eh? The weather? State of the nation ...? I don't care what so long as we're not talking long. That husband'll be home in what — four, five hours? And what I've got in mind'll take all of that!

He tries to embrace her, but again she evades him

Suzy Let's talk about you.
Larry My favourite topic! But save it for later, eh? Much later ... when we sit up in bed: me, if I hadn't given up, smoking my Gauloises, and you, all afterglow and getting ready for seconds ... C'mon, Suzy ...

He pulls her into a kiss

Suzy (*moaning under his mouth*) Larry ...

He pulls her closer, still kissing her

(*Muffled*) Larry, Larry ...
Larry (*muffled*) Suzy ... baby ...

Suzy suddenly pulls free and sits upright

Suzy But that's not your real name, is it?
Larry Huh?! (*He too sits upright to regard her*)
Suzy Larry. It isn't your real name.
Larry Why the hell would you think that!?
Suzy Somebody told me.
Larry Somebody? What somebody? Told you what?

Suzy stands up from the sofa and moves to retrieve her drink

Suzy The Beach Club wasn't the first time I saw you, Larry.

He stares at her — waiting. She takes her "moment", sipping her drink

It was ... four months ago — the Costa Blanca in Altea ... a funny little restaurant where they serve only sea food and you eat with your fingers.

Larry El Guardinos.

Suzy That's it. El Guardinos. You were just leaving — with a girl, of course. You didn't see me, I was with a party of people. One of them recognized you.

Larry Yeah? Recognized me as what?

Suzy He thought you were a man named Holland. "Dutch" Holland. Thought you were a criminal wanted by the British police.

Larry And who was this guy who did all this thinking?

Suzy I don't remember, he was just a casual acquaintance, a tourist we'd picked up *en route*. Ralph! Yes, I'm sure his name was Ralph.

Larry I don't know any Ralph.

Suzy He knew you.

Larry *Thought* he knew me. Ralph? No ... What did he look like?

Suzy What does it matter — if he was mistaken?

Larry That's right. What does it matter?

Suzy I didn't give it a thought at the time, but then, the other day at the Beach Club ... when I saw you again ... You *are* Dutch Holland.

Larry No.

Suzy But I want you to be! Don't disappoint me, Larry, don't let me down now!

Larry Are you crazy? You *are* crazy!

Suzy (*overriding*) All right, all right, it was a mistake. This Ralph, whoever he was, got it wrong and you're not Dutch Holland. But suppose he got it right?

Larry Now look ——

Suzy (*overriding*) I mean it could be possible, couldn't it? We all know that Spain is littered with people like you ... (*quickly, as he might protest*) like Dutch Holland. Thieves and murderers who skipped abroad to where the law can't touch them, and some sit thumbing their noses at authority, while others change their names and burrow deep underground. If you're not Holland, then there's no point in you staying here, there was no point in my picking you up ... and yes, you were right, I *did* pick you up ... for a particular reason — and it wasn't sex!

Larry What then?

Suzy Let's play a game. Let's suppose you *are* Dutch Holland ... (*As he might protest*) Humour me. (*She moves to demonstrate that the oil painting is on a hinge. She swings it aside to reveal a wall safe*) Holland would recognize that, wouldn't he?

Larry Anybody'd recognize it.

Suzy With a *professional* eye. How would a man like Holland go about breaking into a safe like this?

Larry (*intrigued, hesitating for a moment*) This is just a game, right?

Suzy nods and Larry, his curiosity and professional instincts aroused, moves to examine, touch and "case" the safe

Suzy Would he use explosives — blow it open?

Larry He might. But an old tin can like this, I could *tickle* it open in one minute flat! (*He turns to regard her*) If I was Dutch Holland.

Suzy Which you still deny?

Larry Let's keep playing that game. Why would Holland want to bust open that safe?

Suzy To get at what's inside.

Larry Which is?

Suzy Perhaps sixty thousand in notes, uncut diamonds, or both.

Larry (*staring at her, then proffering his glass*) I'll have another drink. A scotch this time. A large one, no water.

Suzy nods, takes the glass, and moves to pour him a large whisky. His eyes never leave her

And carry on with the game.

Suzy I want to leave Alex.

Larry Alex?

Suzy My husband. I've had five years of his dark moods and violent tempers, and him knocking me about — now I want to run! (*She moves back to hand Larry the fresh drink*)

Larry So?

Suzy You don't know him. He's a hard man, ruthless — and clever. He'd see to it that I left with no more than I arrived with — one tatty suitcase, a bright smile and a good and willing body.

Larry But if you could get into that safe ...? (*He drinks*) Sixty thousand, eh? OK, suppose I am Holland, what's to stop me laying you out right now, busting that safe open and ——

Suzy (*interjecting*) Because at this moment, apart from his gun, that safe is empty!

Larry (*stopped dead in his tracks; thoughtfully*) He keeps a gun, eh?

Suzy Alex is a mysterious man. He doesn't confide in me. Officially he's in import-export, but he does deals, I don't know how legitimate they are, but they usually involve cash or the equivalent in diamonds ...

Larry Untraceable.

Suzy Yes.

Larry And he keeps a gun ... maybe he's a "washer woman".

Suzy What?

Larry Laundering hot money.

Suzy Possibly. I don't know. But I do know that, from time to time, that safe holds a small fortune.

Larry You said he didn't confide in you.

Suzy No. But I overhear things, the occasional, furtive phone call ... and sometimes he makes notes ... If you *were* Dutch Holland I'd be your inside man. I'd tell you when.

Larry What would be in it for Holland?

Suzy Half. A straight split.

Larry Yeah? (*He paces away thoughtfully*) Holland could still cross you up — keep a watch on Alex until he feeds that safe ... and then move in solo ...

Suzy If that happened, I'd blow the whistle ... I'd point the finger straight at him.

Larry You've got it all pretty well figured out.

Suzy I've had time to think about it. Ever since I saw you at the Beach Club.

Larry (*sipping his drink, considering*) Where would you run to?

Suzy Somewhere I could lie on a beach for a month or two and work out my life. Perhaps Rio.

Larry (*introspectively*) Rio. (*More forthrightly*) If he's like you say he'd come looking for you.

Suzy That's why I'll go far away.

Larry He'll be looking for a woman on her own — but a *man* and a woman together, it would throw the trail.

Suzy (*staring at him*) You and I ...?

Larry You and Dutch Holland. (*He moves closer to touch her*) I still fancy you, Suzy, maybe even more now I've found out you're my kind of woman. Exactly my kind. Anyway, if this Ralph Whoever made me in Altea, it could happen again here. Maybe it's time I moved on again. And I've never seen Rio. What do you say? It doesn't have to be forever — like you said, a couple of months on a beach, no strings ... it could be fun. Yes?

Suzy (*finally*) Very well — yes.

Elated, he kisses her hard — then finally releases her

Larry OK, Mister Inside Man, when's it to be?

Suzy Tonight.

Larry Tonight!? Hey, wait a minute ——

Suzy (*overriding*) I'm staying with some friends in Torremolinos, it was arranged weeks ago ... so when he gets home I'll be packed and gone — he expects it.

Larry But ——

Suzy (*overriding*) He'll get back here around ten. He'll put the stuff in the safe, and then, he's always tired after these trips, he'll go straight to bed. May even take a pill if he has trouble sleeping. Before I leave I'll slip the catch on the back door — he never checks it — only the front. Then you come in and ... what did you say ... "one minute flat" ...?

Larry What about Rio? We'll have to arrange papers, tickets ...

Suzy I'll meet you in Malaga early tomorrow morning. By the bullring. He'll sleep late, always does, probably won't discover the robbery until noon ... by which time we'll be well on our way to Madrid.

Larry Hold on, let me think about this. If I leave now I could get packed, settle a few things .. and Madrid ...? Yeah, we could lose ourselves in Madrid for a few days — long enough to set up the trip to Rio. Suppose he doesn't put anything into that safe?

Suzy He's going to, I know it. But if he doesn't, if it's empty, you close it up ... sneak away, and we wait for the next time.

Larry You know you're cool, really cool.

Suzy Will you do it!?

Larry Sixty thousand split two ways? Yeah, I'll do it. OK, partner — tonight it is.

CURTAIN

SCENE 2

Later that night

The room is empty and dark. The only sound is the constant buzz of crickets (a sound to set the atmosphere which gradually is lost completely as the action progresses)

After a moment, preceded by the beam of the torch he carries, Larry enters from what we take to be the rear area of the house. He wears a dark jacket now and surgical gloves. He stands utterly still for a moment, playing the torch around the room, then up towards the stairs, and finally to hold on the oil painting

He moves to the desk, pauses again to play the torch back on to the stairs, and then he switches on the desk lamp. He instantly looks back towards the stairs again, but there is no sound

He swings aside the oil painting, regards the safe, flexing his fingers, and then leans close to it and begins to turn the combination knob (or, if the director prefers, he uses a lock picking tool), as he starts to break into the safe. Finally he gives a little sigh of triumph as the door of the safe snaps open. He regards it, and then delves into it, and the first thing he takes out is a shiny revolver. He regards it, hefts it, and then places it down on the desk and delves into the safe again, producing some papers and then a small, soft suede bag with a drawstring. Excitedly he moves back to the light of the lamp and opens the bag, spilling a few uncut diamonds into his palm

Larry is so triumphantly engaged that he does not see Alex entering down the stairs

Alex is of indeterminate age, he might be as young as 35, as old as 45. He need not be a particularly big man, but there is an air of latent strength, of power about him. He looks like a man who might have a violent temper. He wears a robe and is barefoot. He pauses, takes in the scene, then gingerly steps down and reaches to pull one of the Toledo steel daggers from the display

As he does so, Larry senses his presence, spins round, and for a brief, shocked moment they confront each other, unmoving. Then Alex makes a bellowing noise deep in his throat as, dagger raised, he moves in on Larry

As he does so, Larry snatches up the gun from the desk and fires several shots at Alex

Alex is hit, he sways, stumbles, and then falls like a stone to lie still

For a long moment Larry, gun in hand, is frozen, staring at Alex on the floor. Then he is galvanized into action; he snatches up the bag of diamonds, thrusts it into his pocket and starts to rush away. His route must take him within a few feet of Alex, and just as he passes him, Alex startlingly leaps to his feet and grabs Larry from behind. It is so shocking that Larry cries out — then, taking advantage of the shock, Alex easily turns Larry around and slams him hard against the wall or desk—Larry falls to the floor to lie there, stunned and winded. Alex, still holding the dagger, calmly moves to switch on the main lights

Alex Now let's have a look at you. (*He bends to scoop up the fallen gun and break it as he gazes down on the astonished Larry*) Blanks. To scare off an intruder ... just blanks ...

Larry makes a small move and Alex bears in with the dagger

But this is good Toledo steel. You understand what I'm saying? (*In stumbling Spanish*) Habla usted inglese? (*He again bears in with the dagger*) Habla usted ——?
Larry (*interjecting*) I understand you.
Alex You're English! A little bit of free enterprise, eh? The local boys won't like that. (*Then, as Larry might move, the steel returns to Alex's voice, and the dagger to Larry's throat*) Stay right where you are.

Larry freezes and watches as Alex, dagger in hand, never taking his eyes off Larry, backs up to the desk, opens a drawer, delves in, produces a box of ammunition, then quickly puts down the dagger, slips a shell into the gun and snaps it closed

These are the real thing. All right, stand up.

Under the threat of the gun, Larry stands

You have something of mine.

Larry stares at the gun, then pulls the diamond bag from his pocket

Come forward and put it on the desk.

Larry puts the bag on the desk

(*Gesturing with the gun*) Now step away, back to the wall.

Larry goes back to the wall

Put your hands in your pockets, and keep them there.

Larry puts his hands in his pockets, and Alex seems to relax a fraction

That's better. Now who are you?
Larry Santa Claus. I got my dates mixed up!

Alex moves at surprising speed and steps in, slaps Larry hard across the mouth and then instantly steps back and away with the gun trained on him again, leaving Larry holding his mouth

Alex *Who are you!?*
Larry My friends call me Larry.

Alex starts to step in to strike him again

(*quickly*) Holland, Dutch Holland.

Alex regards him and then picks up the diamond bag and tosses it in his hand

Alex How did you know about these?
Larry I didn't, did I? I just struck lucky ... or I *thought* I'd struck lucky. You shouldn't have been here, you should have been tucked up in bed.
Alex I couldn't sleep.
Larry Then you should have taken a pill. *Yeah.*
Alex I was about to. Keep 'em here. (*He pats the desk*)
Larry I didn't know that. That was a bad mistake.
Alex (*regarding him speculatively, suspiciously*) You didn't know about the diamonds? Just a lucky break, eh?
Larry (*ironic*) Oh, yeah. Very.

Larry watches as Alex moves to pick up the phone

You've got your stuff back, no harm done ... Let me go and you'll never see me again.

Alex regards him, then flips over a telephone pad, finds a number and dials it. At no time does he take his eyes off Larry for more than a second or two, or lose his alertness

Alex But I *want* to see you again. At the trial. (*Into the phone*) Policia? This is Alex Winder ... Villa Karibu ... I've got a burglar here and ... (*Listening*) No, Alex Winder. Whine-der. Habla usted inglese? Well is there anyone there who *does*? Whine-der ... Christ, these bloody foreigners!... Look, it's an emergency, *emergencia* ... Whine-der. English. English. Capitan Zachares? Speaks inglese? When does he get back? ... (*Listening*) No, no. No compri. (*Carefully*) Capitan Zachares telephone me, si? *Telefonica*. Si. Si! Numero? Oh, the number ...? Uno, dos ... er ... ocko ... si, si, *ocho*, tres. Si, si. Emergencia, eh? *Whine-der*. (*He hangs up. Then ironically*) Muchas gracia. (*Regarding Larry*) Have you got form in England?

Larry regards him

Yes, you're bound to have — your type — why else would you be here? Well, this one could get you extradited and ——

Larry (*interjecting*) They've got nothing on me back home. Plenty of "sus", yes ... but they couldn't pin anything on me. Not in a million years.

Alex You may wish they could. Have you ever seen a Spanish prison? I've seen the outside of a few, and that's bad enough. On the *inside* ...?

Larry They're going to have to know about the diamonds!

Alex Should that worry me?

Larry I dunno. This ain't Amsterdam and it seems funny having a bag of diamonds and ——

Alex (*interjecting*) Not funny if you deal in them — as I do on occasion. You'd better sit down. But keep those hands in your pockets.

Larry moves to sit down, hands still in pockets

You're a ruthless bastard.

Larry reacts. Alex gestures with the gun

You had the gun, but no "stay where you are", or even a leg wound. No
... four shots right into the chest. I felt the wads hit me. A murdering,
ruthless bastard.

Larry They were blanks.

Alex You didn't know that!

Larry I ... I panicked. You came at me ...

Alex No, you had time. You did it instinctively — second nature. *You
enjoyed it*! (*He stalks around him*) D'you know, I think you've done it
before. Is that what they "can't pin on you back home"? Murder? Is that
it?

Larry Take a walk!

Alex I could if I wanted. And tomorrow I could take another walk ... and
tomorrow and years from now ... Wherever I want — the beach, the bars
... But you? Your walking days are over for a long, long time. You'll be
pacing. To and fro, from locked door to barred window.

Larry Now who's enjoying it!?

Alex Not enjoying. Just ... pointing it out.

Larry You may drop the charges.

Alex Never! Why should you think I might?

Larry I ... haven't thought it through yet. Maybe there's things you don't
know about this heist. Maybe if I told you ... (*Abruptly*) I've got to talk
to a lawyer first.

Alex Talk away all you want. Nothing's going to change those four shots
into the chest — a clear intent to kill. Yes, a ruthless bastard. Murder
comes easy to you ... and you *have* done it before. Haven't you!?

Larry I'll save it for my lawyer.

Alex Let's hope your Spanish is better than mine! (*Pause*) You haven't
offered to buy me off!

Larry reacts

You thought there was something shady about these diamonds, about
me, so why not take the chance and try to buy me off? You never know,
I might be open to an offer. Suppose I said, ten grand and you walk free?!

Larry stares at him

That's what I thought. You don't have it. Times getting hard, are they? All right, I'll make it five,

Larry regards him

Very hard.

The phone rings and again, without taking his eyes off Larry, Alex moves to answer the phone. During the following Larry reacts and stands straight up out of his chair to stare at Alex

Hello? ... Yes, this is Alex Winder. Ah, Captain Zachares! No, no, you don't have to apologize for your men ... I don't speak *their* language either. ... An emergency? ... No, they must have made a mistake, there's no emergency here. I was just making a routine enquiry ... about something that I've since settled. ... No, no, Captain, there's no need for you to come out here ... there's nothing wrong. Nothing wrong at all. Thank you, Captain, sorry to have bothered you. Gracias. ... And buenas noches to you too.(*He hangs up and regards Larry*) What do you know about diamonds?

Larry (*utterly confused*) Huh!?

Alex Diamonds. What do you know about them?!

Larry They're a girl's best friend?

Alex Man's too — better than a dog everytime! (*As he talks, he opens the suede bag and shakes some on to the desk, stirring them with a finger*) They're transportable, concealable, and providing they're right, just a handful can make a man a king. Make all his dreams come true! You didn't strike lucky tonight — on the contrary you were *unlucky*. *These!?* They're flawed, poor quality, the whole shebang of them wouldn't bring more than eight, nine thousand. And that's on the *open* market, but the way you'd have had to dispose of them — underground, through a fence — you'd have been looking at not much more than fifteen hundred. Fifteen hundred pounds, that's what you were prepared to kill for! Small change. Yes, you were out of luck on all counts tonight. While all the luck fell on *my* side. You *are* a ruthless, murdering bastard ... amoral, cunning, quick to kill ... but you see, you're just the man I've been looking for! (*He relaxes, turns his back on Larry and makes his way over to the drinks tray*) Hope you're not a teetotaller?

Larry If I'd sworn off drink on a stack of bibles, I'd want one now!
Alex Gin, vodka ...?
Larry Scotch.

Alex nods and, as he busies himself pouring the drinks, Larry regards his unprotected back, sizing up the situation, and then softly makes to move towards him

Alex (*without turning*) You could try, but you wouldn't make it. (*He turns, gun pointed*) Anyway, don't you want me to satisfy your curiosity? And there's a little matter of fifty thousand pounds I want to give you.

Larry regards him. Alex pockets the gun and moves to hand him a drink

Your wonderful tan has gone a sort of pale yellow. Drive that into you. Cheers.

They drink. Pause

Larry Fifty thousand?
Alex Yes.
Larry You want to *give* me?
Alex Yes.
Larry For why?
Alex Well, certainly not as a gift, that's for sure. No, you will have to earn it.
Larry Earn it?
Alex Yes.
Larry How?
Alex By doing one simple little job for me.
Larry What little job?
Alex Murder my wife.

He finishes his drink, then looks at Larry who is a bit stunned

Better let me top you up — you're definitely starting to look Chinese. (*He takes Larry's glass and moves to pour two more drinks*)
Larry (*finally*) Murder your wife?

Alex Yes. Her name's Suzy. She's quite beautiful really. Very ... sexy ... she'd be your type I think. Yes, you'd like her. I did for a while. But she's a slut. She sleeps around. I can't prove it, but I know she sleeps around. I'm pretty sure there's a new man in her life right now ... she has a kind of ... nervous energy that betrays her. He may even have been here today. I don't know, and frankly I don't care anymore. I just want to be rid of her. Permanently.

Larry Well, I'd say murder definitely comes into that category!

Alex But a bit drastic, eh? Why don't I just divorce her? Yes, that would seem to be the obvious solution, wouldn't it? But you see, I am a cautious man, and even though I *know* she's unfaithful to me, I have no proof ... and she has an animal cunning, oh yes, you have no idea how devious she can be ... how clever. And she has got something on me ... I've got a bad temper ... but I think you already guessed that?

Larry (*fingering his chin*) Yeah.

Alex Unfortunately, I'm quick to lose it too. Something riles me — I just see red and *go*, can't help myself ... I get violent, lash out. I've hit her a few times — not proud of it, but there it is ... and in a divorce court ...?

Larry She might win.

Alex Yes, and I'm not sure how my blood pressure would cope with a huge settlement — not to mention alimony forever more. Anyway, I can't afford it. You see, like you, I'm finding times are hard, and getting harder. The rent on this villa is overdue ... I'm carrying an overdraft and ——

Larry (*interjecting*) You've got a sack of diamonds. Ten grand on the open market, that's what you said.

Alex They're not my diamonds, I'm just the middle man working for a fee. A quite small fee ... and anyway, even if I took the risk, ten thousand wouldn't be enough. I'm in too deep. (*He smiles*) You haven't said no, haven't protested. Yes, murder isn't new to you.

Larry I'm admitting nothing.

Alex But you're still listening.

Larry I liked the sound of that fifty thousand, that's what I liked. It has a nice ring to it.

Alex I want her dead. Out of the way. It would solve everything. I could pretend I just thought of it, but actually it's been in the back of my mind for months now. I've been plotting, thinking up plans, discarding them ... and then tonight *you* came along, and suddenly it's all starting to fall into place. I was getting desperate, was even thinking of doing it myself ... but you, a total stranger ...

Larry ... could end up carrying the can, while you walk free.

Alex Not possible. We would be in it together, there'd be no other way. Each of us would be as involved, as guilty ... as dependent upon the other.

Larry And rich.

Alex (*smiling*) Not just a murdering bastard, but a greedy bastard too!

As Larry bridles at this, Alex holds up placating hands

No that's beautiful ... it's a compliment. What do you think? Will you do it?

Larry You think I'm about to run my neck into a noose without hearing more? You've got a plan?

Alex More or less.

Larry *More or less?*

Alex I know the broad outline, but not the fine details ... but now you are involved ...

Larry Not yet I'm not.

Alex Just keep thinking fifty thousand.

Larry Tell me about this broad outline.

Alex I set up a cast iron alibi. You do the job. We split the proceeds.

Larry Yeah, that's been bothering me, if you're damned near broke, where's this fifty grand coming from?

Alex Her insurance. We took it out when we got married. If she dies, I get more than a hundred thousand.

Larry Ah, *insurance*! D'you know how long it could take them to pay out? Especially if she dies a violent death. I could be waiting *years* for my money.

Alex The minute it's done you'll walk out of here with fifty thousand in diamonds. You won't have to fence them either, I'll show you how and where to dispose of them at their full market value.

Larry I'm still listening.

Alex I said I was getting desperate, that's because sometime, quite soon, I'm going to be in possession of another consignment of diamonds. The biggest I've ever handled. (*He picks up the suede bag and tosses it in his palm*) Not poor stuff like that. Fifty carat, first water, *magnificent* diamonds. And they'll be in that safe for the taking ... for you to take the night we ... *you* do the whole job.

Larry It's going to look like robbery, and along the way Suz ... your wife gets bopped?

Alex Something like that. I'll work it out exactly over the next couple of
   days. Well?
Larry Insurance *and* the diamonds, eh?
Alex Two birds with one stone.
Larry *One* bird. Named Suzy.
Alex Well, are you in? What do you say?

A long pause

Larry I say ... from one murdering bastard to another ...

He extends his hand and they shake hands

CURTAIN

SCENE 3

The following morning

The safe is closed and covered by the oil painting again

Suzy is seated talking on the phone

Suzy Are you sure he's not in the pool?... What about the bar? Have you
   seen him at all this morning?... No, no I've tried his apartment. ... Yes,
   and the hairdressers. ... Look, if he comes in will you ask him to call me?
   Tell him it's urgent. Thanks. (*She hangs up, frets a moment, then makes
   a decision and begins to dial another number when we hear the sound
   of a car coming up to stop outside. She hangs up and opens the door,
   looks off and reacts*) Larry ...?!

Larry enters

Suzy You shouldn't have come here, Alex will be back any moment.
Larry It's Alex I came to see.
Suzy What do you mean? What's going on? I waited for you 'til gone nine
   — when you didn't show I didn't know what to do ... so I took a cab back
   here ... since then I've been trying to call you, I've tried everywhere I
   could think of and ——

Larry (*interjecting*) That's why I couldn't get through. I've been trying to call you.

Suzy For God's sake what happened?! Did I get it wrong? Was the safe empty — was that it? (*Suddenly the thought hits her*) What do you mean, you came here to see Alex?!

Larry Exactly that. He must have been up and about damned early. I found a note pinned to my door — asking me to meet him here.

Suzy Meet him! Oh my God, then he knows about us! Larry, we have to go now — he's dangerous ... unpredictable ——

Larry (*interjecting*) No, he doesn't know about us.

Suzy He must. Why else would he ask you over?

Larry Because of what happened here last night.

She stares at him

How long have we got? Where is he?

Suzy He drove down to the village to get some booze. Larry, what's ——

Larry (*overriding*) Just listen and ask questions later ... if there's time. I came here last night just like we planned, popped the safe, grabbed the stuff and then things went wrong. He caught me.

Suzy Caught you!? But how ——?

Larry (*overriding*) Shut up and listen! He came down to get his sleeping pills. Keeps them right there in the desk. You didn't tell me that, Suzy. You should have warned me.

Suzy Oh, God, I forgot ...

Larry Anyway, first off he was going to hand me over to the local fuzz. And then he didn't. And then he put this deal to me.

Suzy Deal? What deal?

Larry He asked me to kill you.

Suzy stares at him

Suzy Kill ...?

Larry Top you, bop you, *murder* you.

Suzy You're ... joking.

Larry Look at my face. (*Slowly shakes his head*) No joke.

Suzy Kill me ...? But why ... If he doesn't know about us ——

Larry (*interjecting*) Did you know your old man is on the skids and sliding deeper? Near to being skint — B.R.O.K.E. — broke?!

Suzy No ... I told you, he doesn't confide in me ...

Larry Well, he is, and you're his salvation — or a part of it — plus which, and this is the bit that'll break you up, he wants to get away from you as much as you do him! And he's prepared to pay me for the privilege. Fifty thousand — that's a step up from the thirty grand *you* were offering!

Suzy (*pacing away*) Why the ... the ——

Larry (*interjecting*) Bastard is the word we've settled on. *Murdering* bastard.

Suzy (*stopping, turning, and looking at him*) He offered you a deal?

Larry Yeah.

Suzy And what did you say?

Larry We-ll ... you know I have my own kind of morality. I can only be seduced by money! And suddenly he was the highest bidder.

Suzy You agreed to do it?

Larry That's right.

Suzy To murder me.

Larry Yes.

Suzy When does it happen? Now? Are you going to kill me now?

He regards her

No. You wouldn't have told me all about it, if you didn't have something else in mind.

Larry (*grinning*) You know, for someone who doesn't really know me too well, you know me. Sure I said I'd go along — one, it let me off the hook — and two, there's got to be another angle ...

Suzy A more profitable angle?

Larry Yes. Something to exploit.

Suzy How is he going to pay you off? If it's as you say, he's nearly broke, then how is he ——?

Larry (*interjecting*) Your insurance for one thing.

Suzy Insurance?

Larry (*giving a nod*) Says you took it out when you were married. Over one hundred thousand.

Suzy Yes, I remember.

Suddenly she begins to laugh and, for the first time in the scene, Larry is at a loss

Larry Suzy?

Suzy The insurance!

She continues laughing. Larry moves closer

Larry You've got to get a hold of yourself, he'll be back any minute and ——
Suzy (*overriding*) The insurance. You don't know the half of it. (*She moves to the desk, opens a drawer and starts to pull out some papers, scattering them on the desk and searching through them*) I tried to tell him, oh, more than a month ago, as soon as I got the letter, but he was drinking, and in one of his moods. He hit me, blacked my eye, and I never did get to tell him.

Larry moves closer. She now finds the document she was looking for and flourishes it at him

From the insurance company — we didn't keep up the payments ... so the policy has lapsed.
Larry Huh? (*He snatches the document from her to scan it*)
Suzy There *is* no insurance!

Larry stares from her to the document. Then Suzy glances down at the other scattered documents, reacts, picks one up, and looks closer

Suzy Now that's really ironic. *His* is still valid. "Alexander Winder — payable upon death ... one hundred thousand pounds plus profits accrued."

Larry reacts, moves to snatch it from her and study it

Larry I *knew* there would be another angle!
Suzy What do you mean?

We hear the sound of a car approaching, coming up and stopping outside. Larry and Suzy react

Larry Listen, I just got here, right? You don't know me, never saw me before ... Put these away ... (*He shoves the documents across the desk at her*)
Suzy Larry ...?

Larry *Do it*!

She quickly puts the documents back in the drawer — while Larry moves away across to the other side of the room

And for God's sake try to act natural!

Suzy (*composing herself, then whispering across to him*) When can we talk? Shall I meet you at the club?

Larry I dunno. I'll call you later ... and we just this minute met — right?!

The door opens and Alex enters, wearing casual clothes and carrying a cardboard box of booze

Alex Sorry I wasn't here to meet you ...

Larry Just this minute got here.

Suzy You didn't tell me you were expecting anybody.

Alex Wasn't sure myself ... (*To Larry*) Wasn't certain how you'd respond to my note. I'm glad you're here ... (*To Suzy*) Didn't you give him a drink yet?

Suzy That's what you went out to get — remember?

Alex (*opening the kitchen door, entering a pace or two to put down the box of bottles and unpack it*) These are just reinforcements, the place isn't completely dry. You'll have a drink, won't you?

Larry Thanks.

Suzy I'll mix you a spritzer.

Alex No — scotch is his tipple. Made sure I got some more too. (*He leans out of the kitchen to hand Suzy a bottle*) That should keep him going for a while.

Larry I won't be having more than one.

Alex (*still in kitchen*) That's what they all say. The trouble with Spain is that the booze is so bloody cheap — it's too easy not to know when to stop.

Larry I do. I want to keep a clear head.

Alex (*emerging from the kitchen*) Yes, sensible.

Suzy Something *you* might remember.

Alex Not right now. Hot as hell out there and my throat's rasping. Mix me one too, will you?

Suzy I already did.

Larry Now that's nice to see — a thoughtful, caring wife.

Suzy Force of habit, Mr ... er ——?
Larry Just call me Larry.
Alex I suppose Larry hasn't had time to tell you what he's doing here?
Larry } *(together)* { No.
Suzy } *(together)* { Yes.

Alex reacts

Larry *(quickly)* I told her it was business — but not exactly what.
Alex Property development. Larry knows where I could pick up an option on some ve-ry desirable land ... I might invest.
Suzy You have the funds, do you?

Alex and Larry exchange a look

Alex I can raise them. If necessary. If Larry here can convince me. *(To Larry)* You're going to have to go through those facts and figures from top to bottom, and I'm going to ask every awkward question there is, I promise you.
Larry OK by me.
Suzy Do you want me to take notes?

Alex and Larry react and exchange a glance

Alex I thought you'd jump at the chance of having the pool all to yourself.
Suzy I've taken too much sun today.
Alex I see. Yes, it'd be useful if you sat in ... thanks. *(He feels in his pockets)* Oh, damn! Bought myself a pack of cigars and must have left them there, sitting on the counter.
Suzy You have some in the desk ...
Alex No, I smoked the last this morning. I'm out ... darling, would you mind? It'll only take you a few minutes ...?
Suzy All right, give me the keys.
Alex *(handing her the car keys)* Thanks, darling.

Suzy exits

Pause

Larry Why did you ...?

Alex motions him to silence, moving to the door to gaze off. A slight pause, and then we hear the car start up and begin to move away. Only then does Alex relax and turn to face Larry. He pats his pockets, then grins as he produces a small pack of cigars

Alex Well, wouldn't you know — I had them all the time. Poor Suzy's gone on a wild goose chase.

Larry And speaking of wild goose chases ...

Alex You want to know why I sent for you?

Larry Damned right. There was no connection between us before — I was supposed to be the total stranger. Now here I am, sitting here and ——

Alex (*interjecting*) You never were.

Larry (*startled*) Huh?!

Alex A total stranger. It wouldn't work.

Larry Why not?

Alex Think, man! *Because you came up here last night.*

Larry Nobody saw me.

Alex You can't know that for sure.

Larry I was careful. Parked my car down the road and ——

Alex And if someone *did* see you — or your car even ... that would look even worse wouldn't it? If they could testify they saw you coming here furtively, *trying* not to be seen. That'd be tantamount to an admission of conspiracy, wouldn't it!?

Larry regards him, starting to see the logic of this interpretation

This way is better. Open. A casual acquaintance — someone I might be doing legitimate business with.

Larry What kind of business? Property ... I don't know anything about property ...?!

Alex Simpler than that. My car.

Larry Car?

Alex That Renault out there. It's one of the few things around here I actually own! It still belongs to me and I want to sell it. God knows, I thought I was going to have to! You heard about it ... got interested ... and we met a couple of times to haggle over price. What could be more normal?

Larry You're forgetting something.

Alex reacts

Her. Suzy. You rabbited on to her about property deals, and if she tells
them that ... (*He stops dead as he realizes what he has said*)

Alex (*giving a nod*) That's right. She won't be around to tell anyone
anything. Will she? (*He drains his drink, moves to the drinks tray, picks
up the bottle, hesitates, then puts the bottle down again*) Dammit, I *am*
drinking too much! (*He turns back to Larry*) We may not have much
time. That consignment of diamonds could arrive within the next forty-
eight hours — but it doesn't matter, I've got it all worked out now; as
soon as I have those diamonds I'll come back here, put them in the safe.
Then I'll tell Suzy I have to go out again — urgent business — and I'll
make sure she stays here alone.

Larry How?

Alex I'll ... tell her I'm expecting an important call — say she has to stay
in to receive it. I'll bribe her if necessary — tell her there's a fur coat in
it.

Larry That'll be real handy here in Spain!

Alex Well, whatever, I'll think of something. *She'll be here*, don't worry.
Then I'll go down to Pepe's, you know that place on the front?

Larry Yeah, so long as he has a customer, he never closes.

Alex (*giving a nod*) I'll tell him I've had a bust-up with my wife, and then
I'll start to get drunk.

Larry That should be the easiest part for you.

Alex (*regarding him with a hard eye*) I'll pretend to get drunk. Then I'll
make two phone calls. The first will be to you, it'll be your signal to
make your move. I'll tell Pepe I was calling Suzy and she hung up on
me ... and I'll get drunker. Then I'll try again, this time I'll take along
Pepe and whoever else is handy to help plead my cause. We'll all of us
talk to Suzy ... She won't know what I'm on about, of course — she'll
assume I've tied one on again.

Larry And you'll all be able to swear she was alive while you were there.

Alex Then I'll hang up, and get so drunk that I fall down. Pepe won't let
me drive, he'll put me in the back bedroom with his brother — he's done
that before. I'll crash out. Meanwhile ... you ...

Larry I'll be here.

Alex Just like last night. Break in, bust the safe open ...

Larry And along the way, take care of Suzy.

Alex Yes.

Larry What if she's not alone?

Alex Of course she'll be alone ... I told you, I'll leave her here and ——

Larry (*interjecting*) She sleeps around, right? And you think there's a new man in her life. They might take this as a great chance to have it away together.

Larry is enjoying Alex's consternation at this. He is playing with him

Alex Christ! I never thought of that.

Larry If I had to take 'em both out ... wife and lover ... robbery or no robbery, it would look bad for you.

Alex You see, if I'd been going this alone, I'd never have thought of that. Larry, I didn't know how much I needed you until now.

Larry That may be, but what are you going to do about it?

Alex I'll ... I'll tell her I don't know how long I'll be out — could be twenty minutes, might be longer. She won't dare have anyone over then.

Larry You know I'll have to take 'em all, don't you? The diamonds we're going to split fifty-fifty — I'll have to take them all with me when I go.

Alex I know.

Larry You trust me then?

Alex regards him, then holds up his index finger and thumb

Alex About that much! But I have to trust you, don't I? Anyway, you need me to help sell them.

Larry Maybe I don't need you. Maybe I've got my own contacts.

Alex That's possible. In which case ...

Larry Yeah?

Alex I hope you remember that temper of mine — how easily I lose it.

Larry (*grinning*) Hey! We've got to trust each other, right?

Alex Confucius say, "Trust everyone, but cut the cards!" I'll settle for ... we *understand* each other.

Larry Good enough for me.

Alex Seal it with a drink?

Larry No, not for me ...

Alex Come on, I hate drinking alone.

Larry OK — a last one. And small, eh?

Alex nods and moves to recharge their glasses. A slight pause

Alex How will you do it?

Larry Eh? Oh, I hadn't thought yet.

Alex Not the gun?

Larry Uh-uh, a gun has too much to tell to a good forensics man. I dunno
— I guess something hard and heavy. (*He picks up a fire iron out of the
fireplace, holds it, then wields it like a weapon*) Yeah. Quick and easy.

Alex Is that how you did your other murder?

Larry regards him. Alex grins

   Or was it murders? The good old blunt instrument?

Larry (*grinning cockily — it is a story he would like to recount*) No.

Alex Strangulation? A stocking ... *your bare hands*?!

Larry Nothing like that. You'd be surprised if I told you how ...(*He stops*)

Alex (*regarding him*) But you're not going to tell me?

Larry I'm not going to tell you.

Alex Probably best. The less I know, the less I can slip up on. When they
question me ... after ...

Larry Oh, you'll be all right — they'll go easy on you ... bereaved
husband and all that stuff ... and with *your* alibi ...!

Alex What about you, if they start digging around in your background ...?

Larry I learned a long time ago. It's not what they think. It's what they
can *prove*. And I'll make sure I'm as clean as a whistle and whiter than
a lily! You make sure too — lay off the booze — you'll be just
pretending to be drunk, remember?

Alex When they come for me I'll be as sober as a judge ... with a terrible
hangover.

Larry Come for you? That can't be right — who's going to find the body?

Alex hesitates

   Does anybody come here during the day?

Alex A pool man once a week.

Larry You can't rely on him. And that body has to be found pretty fresh,
so they have a better chance of exactly pin-pointing the time of death.
You have to find her.

Alex Yes, I *suppose* that makes sense.

Larry And it's what would happen, isn't it? You tied one on, stayed out all night, and now it's morning, you're a bit ashamed of yourself — you want to get home, make things up as soon as possible.

Alex You're right of course. Yes, that's the way I'll do it.

Larry You bet your life you will! And that's what's at stake here — the rest of your natural!

Alex Stop arguing. I agree — I bow to your superior *past* experience. (*He chuckles*)

Larry looks at him questioningly

I suddenly thought ... if Suzy knew what we were planning ...

Larry That'd stand everything on its head.

Alex Yes. *Yes.* Well, that's it then, we're set?

Larry (*giving a nod*) All I need to know is when.

Alex I should know that soon, by the end of the day perhaps, and the moment I do I'll —

He reacts as we hear the sound of the car approaching, and coming up to stop

(*Quickly; quietly*) I'll call you the moment I know.

Larry (*quietly*) If I'm out — then wait and call again. No notes this time, nothing on paper. Did you like this deal?

Alex Eh?

Larry For her benefit — *the property deal we're supposed to have been discussing*?

Alex Oh ... er ... I'm interested ... but need more information.

Larry OK, I'll —

He is cut short as, off stage, there is the sudden, startling sound of a bomb exploding very close by. If possible, the light effect of the bomb's flash through the windows would be a bonus

Simultaneously, several panes of the leaded glass window fall noisily inwards. And again, if it can be achieved, it would be nice to have, perhaps, a picture suddenly hang awry, a plate fall from the wall and/or an ornament or two fall over. The overall effect is that of the blast of a bomb that has exploded very close by. Like a small earthquake

Larry and Alex are visibly, physically moved by the exploding bomb. They recover their balance but remain in shock for a moment

Alex What the hell was that!?

As one, Larry and Alex start to move towards the door

> *Suzy enters and stands there clutching at the door jamb. Her hair is awry, her face smudged with black, and she clutches her arm*

Suzy Alex, the car ... somebody blew up the car!

They stare at her

> Somebody tried to murder me!

They remain, stunned and shocked

CURTAIN

ACT II

SCENE 1

About an hour later

As the CURTAIN *rises Larry is alone, crouching to pick up one of the broken panes of glass, then putting it down and moving to the open door to gaze off thoughtfully*

Suzy enters down the stairs

Larry You OK now?

Suzy I think so. I took a couple of tranquilizers, but I'm still shaking. (*She extends her hands to display their tremor*)

Larry What happened exactly?

Suzy I've told you ...

Larry Tell me again.

Suzy I ... parked the car in the drive. Got out, closed the door and was nearly at the house when ——

Larry (*interjecting*) Boom!

Suzy (*shaking again*) If it had happened a moment or two earlier ... if I'd stayed in the car a fraction longer ... who did it?

Larry I don't know.

Suzy Was it him? (*With sudden suspicion*) Was it *you*? You bastard, were you in it together?!

Larry Relax. The way things are going, the last thing I want is you dead.

Suzy Then it had to be Alex.

Larry I don't see why. (*He turns to regard the safe/painting*) Unless he's already got those diamonds and didn't tell me.

Suzy Which is possible.

Larry Yeah, it's possible, but it doesn't make sense ... why move without telling me? I'm part of his plan — the lynch-pin. Did you go to the village?

Suzy Yes. Oh, I knew the cigar business was just a ploy so he could talk to you alone, but I went anyway.

Larry And?

Suzy Bought the cigars. I didn't want *him* to know I knew it was a ploy, did I?

Larry Where did you park the car — on the square there?

Suzy No, that was full. The little road off the square.

Larry Maybe that's when they planted the bomb then, unless it was there already ...

Suzy You mean I might have driven all the way there and back, and all the while ...?

Larry Yeah.

Suzy (*shuddering*) Don't.

Larry They may have done it right in your own driveway.

Suzy But *who*?

Larry I dunno. Your husband's a mysterious man — shady — you said so yourself ... Man like that can make enemies. Yeah, I reckon that bomb was meant for him — not you. You look all in.

Suzy I feel it. Delayed shock ...

Larry What you need is a drink.

Suzy No. Drink and the pills ... I'd fall down.

Larry Maybe that'd be best. Lie down, get some sleep. Yeah. (*He moves to pour her a drink*)

Suzy It all seemed so simple yesterday — is that when it was — only yesterday? It seems an age away. We should be in Madrid now, just a step away from Rio ... *it was all so damned simple*! Now it's fallen down around our ears. What do we do now? What do *I* do? Sit around and wait for him to murder me?

Larry Not him. (*He hands her the drink*)

She stares at him

C'mon, drink up.

She stares at the glass she holds

Suzy And ... when I'm fast asleep ... a pillow over my face and ——

Larry That's a great idea. But it's not what's going to happen.

Suzy Then what *are* we going to do?

Larry Back track, turn the whole thing on its head — reverse the plan.

Suzy Reverse?

Larry Look, you're not insured anymore, are you? *But he still is!* Think about it.

Suzy Larry ...?

At this moment we hear a car approaching to eventually stop outside

Larry (*urgently*) Drink! And soon as he gets here, you go and lie down, I want some more time alone with him. *Go on!*

Suzy drinks. We hear the car door slam

Alex (*off*) Thanks for the lift, Captain!

Alex enters

Jesus, these Spanish police! You'd think with tourism propping up their economy the way it does, they'd learn just a few words of English! If that Captain Zachares hadn't turned up I'd still be there! (*He homes in on the drinks tray and starts to pour himself a drink*)

Larry What happened?

Alex Forms to fill in, questions, more questions, more forms — and every one in triplicate, my wrist aches from signing!

Larry What did they say about your car getting blown up?

Alex A bomb. They're towing away the wreckage now.

Larry Well, of course it was a bloody bomb, soon as I heard it I knew ... but who planted it? And why?

Alex The work of that separatist group.

Larry Terrorists!? But why aim at you or Suzy? I know they sometimes pop off a firecracker on the beach ——

Suzy (*interjecting*) But always with plenty of warning first.

Larry That's right. They know about that economic tourist prop too. Why you? Why would they try to hit a foreigner?

Alex Ah, that puzzled the illustrious Spanish cops too. At least, I presume they were puzzled, I couldn't understand a damned word they were saying. But then the good Captain Zachares came on the scene ... and ...

Larry And?

Alex He was just as flummoxed. It was I who eventually came up with the answer. Yes, I suddenly realized that I drive a white Renault — and so too does the local mayor.

Suzy You mean it was a mistake? They were actually going after the mayor ...

Alex *(interjecting)* And got the wrong car. Yes, that's how it would *seem*.

Larry Seem? You mean you have doubts?

Alex I'm thinking about it. *(He regards Suzy)* Suzy, my dear, after what's happened — or nearly happened, don't you think you should get some rest?

Larry She was just going to. Took a couple of pills — I persuaded her to wash 'em down with a drink ...

Suzy Yes, I ... I feel a bit woozy now. I think I will. *(She moves to the stairs — then pauses)* Hope to see you again, Larry.

Larry You will.

Suzy exits up the stairs

Larry moves to look upstairs and make sure she has gone, then turns to Alex

You've got a glint in your eye.

Alex And a spring in my step. Well, don't you see this provides us with the one element we were always missing? A Number One Suspect. Or suspects.

Larry This separatist group ...?

Alex Yes. And we get the plus of a motive.

Larry stares at him — Alex moves to swing aside the painting to reveal the safe

Funds. Those people are always hungry for funds to fuel their cause. Don't they knock over the occasional bank or army payroll? Then why not my diamonds?!

Larry Now wait a minute, the cops already eliminated you as a victim. When you pointed out that your car and the mayor's ——

Alex *(interjecting)* Yes, and I could have bit my tongue the moment I said it. Because a second later it all became blindingly clear — the whole plan just fell into place. If I hadn't mentioned the car ... but it's not irretrievable — it just means a little more setting up.

Larry For what?

Alex To persuade the cops that I *was* the intended victim. Then, when you break open the safe and Suzy is dead ... they'll lay the whole thing at the terrorists' door.

Larry They'll deny it.

Alex They might. But then who'll believe them — a group that has already murdered a number of innocent people? On the other hand, they might just *claim* responsibility. It might suit them to ... and hand us a nice free gift!

Larry OK, OK, that's neat — I buy that ... but how do we bring the cops back around to thinking it was you they were after all the time?

Alex I would have thought that obvious. Another attack!

Larry reacts

(*Pacing away*) Not here at the house, don't want them concentrating too much attention up here ... The boat!

Larry What boat?

Alex I have a small speedboat moored in Marbella. Been trying to sell it for a couple of months now, but luckily I didn't find a buyer ... It's still there, and perfect for our purpose. I could creep down there, open the cocks, knock a few holes in the hull — sink her.

Larry That doesn't sound too dramatic — or like terrorists.

Alex All right then, I'll douse it with petrol — set light to it ...

Larry Too risky. You have to be there to do that.

Alex Then what do you suggest?

Larry A bomb. That's their trademark, isn't it? A nice, big bang.

Alex And where the hell would I get a bomb? I know absolutely nothing about ——

Larry (*interjecting*) From me. I'll make you one.

Alex You're kidding me. A bomb? I don't know much about them, but I *do* know that you need explosives, detonators ... a timing device!

Larry Sure you do — but you'd be surprised how many of those things can be found in the average household — or garden shed. There's certain kinds of weedkillers will explode if you know how to handle them. A detonator ...? Can be a base of a shotgun shell ... and a timer can be anything from a cheap alarm clock to a five quid calculator!

Alex (*staring at him*) You *are* kidding me.

Larry Sometimes you don't need any of that. Sometimes you can rig an explosion out of the means at hand. (*He moves to look briefly at the gas artificial log fire*) Why, I could pull this room down around your ears right now!

Alex stares at him

Listen, I started out as a safe man — that was my apprenticeship. Along the way you get to handle "jelly", nitro, plastics ... Bombs? Explosions? They're my speciality!

Alex (*pointing at wall safe*) You didn't blow that safe.

Larry I didn't have to ! *That* safe? All I had to do was *breathe* on it! But if it'd been Weston "Master Lock" ... or one of the Banham range say ... I'd have blown it.

He turns to see Alex still regards him sceptically

You don't believe me?

Alex I'd like to.

Larry I don't do safes much anymore, not as a rule. I escalated to ... other things. Top man in my field. A "bang man" they call me.

Alex What the devil is a "bang man"?

Larry (*grinning*) Nothing to do with my sex life! Listen, do you remember the Prentice case?

Alex Prentice? No.

Larry Just over two years ago. He was a customs officer — and chief witness in a drugs case — was all set to send a parcel of top dealers down the river. Then he didn't.

Alex Andrew Prentice! Yes, I do recall ... but he died in a fire, didn't he, not an explosion? I know that — at the time — there were some unanswered questions, but ... (*He stops and regards Larry*) were you involved in that?

Larry (*hesitating, his earlier bravado replaced with caution*) It was the sort of thing I *might* have done. My kind of work.

Alex A "bang man"? Who's going to make me one bomb?

Larry Nothing too big. We just want to take out your boat, not the whole marina.

Alex How long will it take you to make it?

Larry You'll have it tonight. Any news on the diamonds?

Alex I'm expecting a call anytime now. Soon as I get it, I'll let you know.

Larry It'll be soon then?

Alex Very soon.

Larry OK, I'll see you later. With the bomb. (*He moves to the door, then*

pauses) I can't be the guy who's thinking of buying your car anymore. You don't have one. You'll have to think of something else.
Alex Yes.
Larry Something clever.

Larry exits

Alex (*gazing after him; thoughtfully*) I will. I'll think of something diabolically clever.

We hear the car start up and move away

Alex moves to the desk, opens a drawer and carefully takes out what is unmistakeably a small explosive device — wires linked to a bundle of dynamite sticks — and the clear dial of a timing device. He smiles, turns a switch and the device starts to tick loudly

CURTAIN

(NB If, on discussion, this action is considered to be giving away too much too soon, then it could be deleted, with the CURTAIN falling after Alex's last line)

SCENE 2

Later that evening

The room is empty, and we hear a car approaching to come up and stop at the house

Alex enters down the stairs and moves to the front door, just in time to open it as Larry enters, carrying a small valise

Alex Did you bring it? Is that it?
Larry Where's your wife?
Alex Only just woken up, she's taking a bath. Did you bring it?

Larry Yeah, I brought it. (*He moves to place the valise on the desk, unzip it and bring out a small explosive device*)

Alex That's it? It doesn't look much.

Larry It'll do the job.

Alex How does it work?

Larry Simple. See this kitchen timer? You set it for anything from one to thirty minutes. (*He turns it and it starts to tick*) Then this switch here ...? Throw it and it's armed. I've taped it down so there can't be any accidents *en route*.

Alex That's it?

Larry That's it. (*He places the device down on the desk*) You'd better plant it — I don't want to make myself obvious looking for your boat.

Alex I'll do it. (*He glances at his watch*) I'll do it now. (*He snaps his fingers*) How do I get there? I don't have a car ... tried to rent one, but they won't have anything until tomorrow.

Larry You'd better take mine. (*He offers the keys*) I'll wait for you here. (*He picks up the device and proffers it to Alex*) Plant it deep as you can in the hull — close to the gas tank.

He reacts as he sees Alex makes no move to take the device

Alex You're not wearing gloves. It must be covered in your prints.

Larry (*grinning*) Listen, when this goes — over water too — there isn't going to be anything left to find a print on!

Alex Nevertheless, I'll wipe it off before I plant it. (*He produces a handkerchief to receive the device*)

Larry Suit yourself.

He thrusts the device into the valise, and hands the valise to Alex

Alex I was going to have to go into town anyway.

Larry (*reacting*) The diamonds ...?

Alex (*giving a nod*) Are on their way — be handed over to me about an hour from now.

Larry So we have to do it soon?

Alex I thought — tomorrow night — after this little bang has sunk into the Spanish cops' consciousness ... tomorrow night would be perfect.

Larry I'll cancel all my other engagements! OK, you'd better get going.

Alex nods and, carrying the valise, heads for the door

And be careful with my car, d'you hear? It's not paid for yet!

Alex exits

During the following action we hear the car start up and move away

Larry moves to regard the painting. He hinges it aside, runs a loving hand over the safe, then flips the painting back into place again

Suzy enters down the stairs

Suzy Larry! I just saw your car leaving and I thought ——
Larry (*interjecting*) Alex took it.
Suzy To go where?
Larry Into town.
Suzy What for?
Larry To set up phase one.
Suzy Phase one?
Larry Of the plan to murder you.

She regards him. Pause

Suzy I slept the whole day away.
Larry He told me. You look better for it.
Suzy I ... I had a bad dream. About us. A nightmare. I dreamed that you suggested that we ... kill Alex.
Larry It was no dream. I didn't actually come out and say it, but it's what I have in mind.
Suzy Larry ——
Larry (*overriding*) Come on, see sense — it was *him* brought the word murder into this game. What are you going to do ...? Sit back and wait for it to happen?
Suzy You said you wouldn't go through with it.
Larry Suppose I don't, suppose I walk away? Then what? D'you think he's going to forget it? It's stuck in his mind now and someday he's going to do it — with or without me! But my way, we take everything he's planned and turn it against him. And along the way we both get to be rich ... and sit in that Rio sun, eh?

Suzy But ... murder ...

Larry Self-defence! We get everything — the diamonds, insurance money ... and you get to be free. No running, no looking over your shoulder.

Suzy *If* we got away with it.

Larry We will. Courtesy of Alex Winder. He set it up, primed the gun — we just point it at a different target, that's all.

Suzy The insurance would make me a suspect straight away.

Larry Not the way Alex has it figured.

She regards him

You know where he is now? Planting a bomb on that boat of his.

Suzy A bomb! That's crazy — why would he want to destroy his own boat?

Larry To persuade the cops they were wrong — it wasn't the mayor those terrorists were after — it was Alex all along.

Suzy I see. So now, if Alex *were* to be killed ...

Larry The finger would point at them.

Suzy That's clever.

Larry But he is. Too damned clever for his own good. Well? You coming around to my way of thinking?

Suzy The insurance ... they'd dig deep ... I'd still come under suspicion ...

Larry The way I've got it planned, there's no way you could possibly have done it. Suzy ...?

Suzy (*a sudden thought*) A bomb? Where did Alex get a bomb?

Larry From me. I made it for him.

Suzy Will it work?

Larry Work?! Listen, that's my trade ——

Suzy (*interjecting*) And he's got it with him now?

Larry Yeah.

Suzy Then why didn't you booby trap it? If it's your trade, you could have done that, couldn't you? Why didn't you set it to kill him while he's at the marina? While you and I have the perfect alibi ...?

Larry Think it didn't cross my mind? The reason I didn't do it is because that safe is empty. Because of the diamonds! Anyway, what I've cooked up is better — safer.

Suzy And just what have you got cooked up?

Larry It happens here. With you as a witness ...

Suzy But if I'm actually here ——

Larry (*overriding*) Hear me out. Alex plants his bomb, right? There's a big bang, goodbye boat, and the cops think terrorist — they think of Alex as a target. Alex gets back here with the diamonds ...

Suzy reacts

Yes, he's picking 'em up today. He puts them in the safe — and then he tells me to go ahead — and kill you tomorrow night.

Suzy But you don't.

Larry Could I ever?! But I say yes, I go along. The plan is, he leaves here at say ... around seven ... goes to a bar in town, gets drunk, stays the night there.

Suzy The cast iron alibi?

Larry Right! Meanwhile, I break in, steal the diamonds ——

Suzy Why?

Larry Because that's what this is all about for Christ's sake!

Suzy But if you're a terrorist ——?

Larry (*interjecting*) Why do I steal? To fund the cause. That's Alex's idea, and it's a darned good one. We're going to use it. Where was I? Oh, yeah ... *I* steal the diamonds ... while *you*, alone in the house, hear something ... come down to investigate — and I bop you. Bop you so hard that you stay bopped. Forever.

Suzy That's the plan?

Larry What your dear devoted husband thinks I'm going to do. Yes.

Suzy And what do you have in mind?

Larry Some subtle changes. First off I'm going to be here *before* Alex leaves. I'll park my car behind that villa on the road up. It's shuttered and empty — no-one there to see me. Then I'll walk — the back way over the rocks, it'll take me maybe half an hour, but the exercise'll be good for me.

Suzy And then?

Larry Then I sneak in here ... and take him out.

Suzy Take him ——?

Larry (*interjecting*) I kill him. Hit him hard ... with this maybe ... (*He moves to pick up a fire iron from the fireplace and slap it into his palm*) Yeah, as they say, "this'll do nicely". I'll rough up the room, make it look as though there was a fight ...

Suzy There might well be if you're not careful. Alex is a powerful man.

Larry Don't I know it! No, I'll get him from behind ... he'll be full of himself — elated ... won't suspect a thing ... and then ... (*He mimes several heavy blows with the fire iron*)

Suzy stares at him. There is a small, profound silence

Then I'll tie you to this chair ... (*He moves to swing the chair by the desk around a few inches*) I'll tie you really tight, but don't worry, I'll drag him over behind the desk, you won't have to sit looking at him all night.
Suzy All night!?
Larry That's going to be the tough part for you. I'll delay tying you long as I can ... but whatever way you look at it, it's going to be a long night. When I leave, you'll be tied here, the safe'll be open, the diamonds gone .. and Alex will be dead. You getting the picture? When you're found and released your story will be this ... That evening two men burst into the villa — both masked, both Spanish. Only one of them spoke a smattering of English. They grabbed you, slapped you around, then tied you to the chair and started busting the safe ... when I do it I'll make it a clumsy, amateur job. They thought you were alone, but your husband — Alex — was upstairs sleeping off a late siesta and a couple too many brandies. He suddenly came down, surprised them, and one of them took this to him ... (*He gestures with the fire iron*) They killed him, grabbed the diamonds from the safe, and took off, leaving you here. It's as simple as that, Suzy.

Suzy does not move for a moment, then she does, to look at the chair

Suzy I'm going to be tied there. Really tight?
Larry You have to be — for your own protection — no way must they be even able to *think* that you tied yourself. It's the best alibi you can ever have. How *could* you have killed him, tied like that?
Suzy For how long?
Larry Huh?
Suzy How long do I have to be tied there?
Larry Next morning.
Suzy Who's going to find me? Hardly anyone ever comes up here ... I could stay there, tied and ——
Larry (*interjecting*) I'll arrange that. It has to be the cops who find you ... find the whole scene ... they have to see those ropes for themselves.
Suzy You'll arrange that?

Larry Yes.

Suzy How?

Larry Again, courtesy of Alex. This terrorist thing works for us from all angles. Does Alex water ski?

Suzy Water ski?! No.

Larry Good. I do. I'm terrific too — told you, I never do anything I'm not good at. Recently I've been giving the odd lesson, to make myself some eating money — that's why I've been up here recently ... helping Alex get into shape. Day after tomorrow. I've got a lesson lined up for Alex — early. He's cancelled a business meeting and paid me in advance. Now he doesn't show up. I'm worried. I heard about his car ... and then how they blew up his boat, so I'm really worried. I keep trying his phone, and it rings, but he doesn't answer. Now I'm really *very* worried. So I call the cops ... they'll react ... and they'll have someone out here right away to check it out. And there *you* are ... and there *he* is ...

Suzy regards him. Long pause

I don't think they'll lean on you hard — not under the circumstances ... you can just cry ... break up. You don't have to make much sense at all. Then later — we-ll, by that time they'll know for sure you couldn't have done it, and they'll just be ... respectful and sympathetic ... to the bereaved widow ... and go off chasing after terrorists! Can you do it? I'm relying on you, Suzy.

Suzy The Rio trip will be out for a while ...

Larry No more than a week or two. Me? They won't have any interest in me, I'll be able to take off whenever I want ... and I will with the diamonds. And you ...? First off, forget the insurance.

Suzy What?!

Larry You haven't thought of it — you're too shocked and grief stricken ... maybe you don't even know there *is* insurance. You decide to go away, get as far as you can from this unhappy memory. Let the insurance people find you, they've got to do that sooner or later. So you take off — to some far flung shore. Like Rio. And I'll be waiting for you. All you have to get through is that night and those few hours after the cops bust in here. Can you? Will you?

Suzy I can do it. But how about you, Larry?

Larry Me? All it's going to take is a few yards of rope — and this. (*He slaps the fire iron into his palm again*)

The phone rings. Larry and Suzy are momentarily startled, and then Suzy moves to pick up the phone

Suzy Hello? Alex! Yes, he's here. (*She turns to Larry*) It's Alex. Wants to talk to you.

Larry (*frowning; taking the phone*) Yeah? You're there already? You made good time. ... Yes, I know it's a good, fast car. ... Yes. Yes, I see. ... Yes, I'll take a look if I can. ... Right, see you later. (*He hangs up*) He sounds drunk.

Suzy What else is new?

Larry When would he have had time?

Suzy He carries his own. A little flask. Aptly covered in *snakeskin*!

Larry I hope he doesn't get careless now ... Start lousing things up when we're this close!

Suzy What did he want?

Larry For my ears only, you're not supposed to know.

Suzy But you're going to tell me, aren't you?

Larry He said to go out on to the terrace and watch the moon come up.

Suzy Moon? It's on the wane and ——

Larry (*interjecting*) The moon over the marina!

Suzy regards him, then Larry reacts (NB We could hear the muffled, far off sound of an explosion, or could just let it play on Larry's heightened perceptions)

You hear that?

Suzy What? I didn't hear anything.

Larry Neither did I. But I felt it — through the soles of my feet. Explosion. Christ he was quick!

Suzy looks at him — then rushes away to exit out of the door

Larry remains, then moves to pour himself a drink

After a pause, Suzy enters through the door again, to remain there staring at him

Suzy There was a bright light — a fire — down by the marina. It's dying away now.

Larry Uh-huh. It would.

Suzy (*moving to him*) The moon ...?

Larry That was no moon, that was phase two. (*He regards her*) We're going to do it, aren't we? Just the way I said?

Suzy (*finally nodding*) Yes, we're going to do it.

Larry (*lifting his glass in a toast*) To phase three then.

Suzy Final and absolute.

Larry In it together all the way.

Suzy All the way. 'Til death us do ... (*stopping as she realizes what she is saying*)

Larry (*regarding her*) Just one death. His. Tomorrow night. (*He drinks*)

CURTAIN

SCENE 3

Later that night

The radio is on, from which an operatic aria plays— something of great, tragic power, starting softly at first, but then rising until it is blasting out

Alex is seated in the chair by the desk, slumped into it, in an attitude of despair, staring at nothing in particular. On the desk before him is the valise. Nearby is a half-full bottle of whisky

We hear a car coming up to eventually stop outside. Alex does not react to this, but just sits, staring, then reaches out a hand for the bottle and is just swigging from it when there is a banging at the door — and then it is slammed open

Larry enters to stand there, gazing in for a moment at Alex, and then switches off the radio

Larry OK, what's this all about? (*He strides over to grab Alex's wrist and push the bottle down from his mouth. Then, without raising his voice*) You called me. You said urgent. Why? For Christ's sake when we're this close ... If you start fouling things up now! You drunken sot ... did you get the days mixed up, is that it? We agreed tomorrow night ...

Alex I'm sorry ... sorry ...

Larry Just tell me why you called. Why you dragged me out of bed ...?

Alex I had too many. I was so ... so *happy*. Larry, you've got to help me ...

Larry Keep your voice down, you'll wake Suzy.

Alex Suzy. Suzy ... (*He seems close to tears*)

Larry Get a hold of yourself ... Christ, you were OK when I left here this evening. What happened?

Alex Told you. Had too many. Was happy ... we were so close, Larry ... so close.

Larry What's going on here? And will you keep it down ...?! If she wakes up ...

Alex She won't. She won't ever wake up.

Larry What are you saying ...? What about Suzy? Where is she?

Alex She's dead.

Larry Huh? What do you mean, she's dead? She can't be dead!?

Alex Dead. Dead. It was all going so well ... I could see the future, stretching away.

Larry *What do you mean, dead*?! How? Where? (*He grabs the front of Alex's shirt*) Listen to me! Where—is—Suzy?

Alex There. (*He waves a hand that encompasses everything*)

Larry Where? Show me!

Alex regards him, then lumbers to his feet and moves to open the kitchen door. We get a restricted view in, but we can see Suzy's legs — the upper half of her covered by an old apron — and the overall impression is that the formerly pristine white kitchen is now red with blood: on the walls, the tiles, flecked on Suzy's body

Alex stands in the doorway, subtly barring the way to Larry, who looks in for a long moment, and then he turns away to lean against the door jamb

Jesus Christ!

Alex gazes into the kitchen for a long moment, and then closes the door again

Alex I'm sorry, Larry ... sorry ...

Larry Why, why, why!? It wasn't supposed to be this way, you know it wasn't supposed to be this way. Why ... how for Christ's sake?!

Alex It was soon after you left. I told you, I was happy. I ... I wanted to celebrate. In anticipation. I had a few. And Suzy kept looking at me. Never saw her look at me quite that way before ... she was ... triumphant. As though she was saying, "I know something you don't know." I never saw her like that before. Smiling, enigmatic ... I looked at her and kept thinking, "All right, smile you bitch ... because soon you'll be dead." I kept seeing her dead. Then she said something. I ... I can't recall just what ... but it riled me ... I shouted at her ... and she just stood there ... there by the fire ... holding this ...(*he picks up the fire iron*) swinging it between her hands. Smiling ... "I know something you don't know!" I'm not sure what happened or how it happened ... I snatched this from her ... She was scared then — that smile slipped from her face then. She ran into the kitchen ... I followed her. I was still holding this. I don't know how many times I hit her. I must have blanked out for a while then.

Larry (*holding the fire iron*) This?

Alex I just saw red ... it happens to me. Then, soon as I realized that she was ... realized what I'd done, I called you.

Larry You hit her with this?!

Alex Yes.

Larry tosses the fire iron to the ground

Larry ...?

Larry You stupid bastard. You ruined everything!

Alex No, Larry, that can't be. We've come so far, so near ...

Larry Bastard, bastard!

Alex I ... need you more than ever now, Larry. I carried the ball until now, plotted the moves ... now ... I'm in your hands. Larry ...?

Larry paces away — opens the kitchen door — angrily looks in again. Alex moves to grab at him

Larry? What are we going to do?

Larry (*slamming the kitchen door shut again*) I'm thinking about it! (*He paces away*)

Alex (*watching him anxiously*) What's changed ...? She was going to end up dead, wasn't she? And right here ... and probably beaten with something like that ... what's so different?

Larry The timing. And we weren't prepared, that's another thing. And you here when it happened — your alibi — that's what's different! It's all different! Not what I planned at all! You're on the spot now — out in the cold on your own.

Alex But we're in this together.

Larry Not this. I never agreed to this! Why the hell couldn't you hold on to your temper for just one more day?! We'd have been home and dry.

Alex The drink, I shouldn't have been drinking ... I couldn't help myself.

Larry ...?

Larry turns away

I'm sobering up now. Starting to think clearly.

Larry Well, that's great news.

Alex I'll do anything you say. I've got the diamonds, Larry, they're in the safe — a hundred thousand pounds worth in stones, that hasn't changed. We can still do something, can't we? You can salvage something out of this mess?

Larry Salvage?!

Alex You're the expert ... you can surely come up with ——?

Larry (*interjecting*) Will you just shut up yapping a moment and let me think! (*Pacing away*) The road was empty on the way up here, didn't pass a soul.

Alex You wouldn't. Not tonight. They have a fiesta in Mijas. A flamenco show, dancing in the square ...

Larry I saw some cops prowling in the village — more than usual but I'm clean. That's something ... not much, but something.

Alex If you hadn't turned up I ... I was going to take her to the ravine, toss her in, make it look as though she fell ... then scrub out the kitchen, and ——

Larry (*interjecting*) You don't touch her, you don't move her an inch — and don't go near that kitchen again. Neither of us will. That's where it happened — forensics'll prove that, and that's fine by me. It fits.

Alex Fits? You *do* have another idea ——

Larry (*interjecting*) Do you have any rope, strong rope?

Alex No, but there's some gardening twine ——

Larry (*interjecting*) Not good enough. How about ties ...

Alex Ties!?

Larry Yeah. Neckties — you've got neckties, haven't you?

Alex (*puzzled*) Yes.
Larry (*interjecting*) Fetch 'em — about half a dozen will do.

Alex nods and turns to go

But before you go — open the safe!

Alex stops, hesitating

You'll do anything I say — remember?

Alex moves to swing aside the painting and (either with key or combination) opens the safe, swings it aside — then turns to regard Larry

(*Reminding him*) Half a dozen ties. Any colour will do.

   Alex exits up the stairs

Larry moves to the safe — delves in, eagerly produces a suede drawstring bag and moves to open it and spill the contents on to the desk — a quantity of brightly sparkling cut stones. Larry happily sifts them with his finger, and then carefully scoops them back into the bag again, and puts it into his pocket. Then he glances back at the safe and, on impulse, delves in and produces the revolver. He hefts it

Alex enters down the stairs, carrying some ties

Alex Careful — it's loaded — with live shells this time.
Larry (*grinning*) Thanks for telling me.
Alex These OK?
Larry They'll do fine. Sit in the chair.

Alex frowns, but sits in the chair indicated

   Put your hands behind you.
Alex What are you going to do?
Larry Tie you up.

Alex reacts, jerking around in the chair to look at Larry. Grim faced, Larry points the gun at Alex. Then he grins and lowers the gun

You've got to really trust me now, Alex. I'm all you've got.

Alex still stares at him

OK, here's the picture. Two terrorists — Spaniards — burst in here.
They're both masked; one has a smattering of English. They grab you,
tie you to the chair — then rough you up until they make you tell them
where the key to the safe is. (*NB If a combination safe is used, the
dialogue should read, "make you tell them the combination to the
safe".*) You do. They open it, take the diamonds and then, just about that
time Suzy, your wife, returns from her walk ... unexpectedly. She
surprises them — she screams, they panic, she runs into the kitchen still
screaming ... one of them follows ... carrying *that* (*the fire iron*). He hits
her once, twice, a few times. She's dead. They run. You're still here, tied
so tight that there is no way you could have done it. In a day or two we
meet and split up the diamonds.
Alex Larry ... that's terrific!

And he eagerly thrusts his hands out to be tied

Larry Behind you.

*Alex puts his hands behind him, and Larry moves to start tying him to
the chair*

It's not a bad plan for spur of the moment.

He pulls a tie very tight and Alex grunts

Sorry, but it's got to be so tight the cops can no way think you somehow
did it to yourself.
Alex That's all right. Tighter the better. It's my alibi. I knew I could rely
on you to come up with something, Larry. And it'll work, won't it?
Nothing overlooked.
Larry It'll work just fine. (*He pulls the last tie very tight and steps back*)
How's that?
Alex (*struggling ineffectually*) I'm tied all right. You're a clever bastard,
Larry.

Larry Aren't I though? Oh, one more thing ... (*He suddenly strikes Alex hard across the face a couple of times*) They roughed you up — remember — to make you open the safe? It's got to look good.

Alex So now we're even.

Larry Yeah. This gun ...? Have you got a licence?

Alex (*hesitating*) No.

Larry I'd better keep it then. Don't want the cops finding it, and getting curious. (*He pats his pocket*) And I've got the diamonds too.

He turns then and playfully aims the gun at Alex, who tenses

It would be so easy.

Alex You wouldn't.

Larry Why not?

Alex You need me alive to tell them about the terrorists ... shoot me now, and it could be just a robbery ... start them thinking. Anyway, you don't trust guns — tell too much to forensics.

Larry Then maybe I'll just leave you here, take the diamonds and blow.

Alex You could, but you know I'd come after you ... wouldn't stop until I found you.

Larry Yes, that's what I thought, you'd never give up. Well, only one way left now.

Alex Do me a favour before you go. (*He nods towards the bottle on the desk*) A drink.

Larry Sure.

Larry moves to pick up the whisky bottle, returns to Alex who tilts his face to receive a swig from the bottle, but, unexpectedly, Larry shakes/ pours the whole contents of the bottle over Alex's face, clothes, and the ties securing him

Larry Say when!

Alex (*coughing and spluttering*) What the ...!?

Larry turns away, moves back to the safe, closes it, and hinges the painting back into place

Larry You said it, Alex old boy. Yes, you'd come after me ... and you might just find me. I can't take that chance. That's why this is goodbye. (*He turns to look at Alex's face and grins*) Change of plan. No Spanish terrorists — just you and Suzy. And me. Let me tell you about it and, well, if you can poke a hole in it, maybe I'll think again. The safe's locked and closed — there was no break in. It was also empty — no diamonds. You see, Alex, I'm betting that the only people know about those diamonds are you ... and whoever you're working for ... and if I'm right, I don't think they'll be making any complaints to the cops. Oh, they may start their own investigation — but where are they going to look? For who? When you talked to them you never mentioned me, did you? The guy who was going to help you rip them off!? No, you never mentioned me.

He now moves to start firmly closing any windows that are open, and takes a cushion off the sofa and wedges into the window with the broken panes. Then he moves to pick up the knife from the desk, moving towards Alex, who can only stare at him in utter consternation

This furniture came with the villa, right? Yeah. Let me show you something ... (*Suddenly he moves to the sofa and slices into it with the knife. [NB Staging should actually conceal the cut he is making, and the actor's body could screen him tearing away a small strip of Velcro to fake the noise of the cut.] Then he delves into the cut, comes up and turns, holding out a handful of the stuffing*) Looks good on the outside. But inside? It's cheap. Look at this stuff — synthetic. (*He moves to the desk, puts the small amount of stuffing into an ashtray and then strikes a match and puts it to the stuffing, which instantly burns bright and fierce, and is quickly consumed.*) It burns like a crematorium oven. And that's pretty close to the truth, Alex old boy. (*He quickly strides over and pushes the chair close up to the sofa, then pulls the gun from his pocket*) Yeah, I could use this on you, but like you said — forensics. No, a man should stick to what he knows best. To his own trade. (*He moves to pick up the three-branched candelabra and places it firmly on the desk. Then he carefully lights each candle, watches them sputter, then take and burn brightly*) His own trade, Alex! The "bang man". I told you once I could rig a bomb out of the means at hand — well, now I'm going to prove it to you.

Alex Prove ...?

Larry You know the tough part of being a bomber? Going to the job — if you get unlucky and someone stops you for a routine check and you're carrying caps and wires and explosive. What do you say — you're going to a Guy Fawkes party?! Sometimes you have to do it, sometimes it's the only way. But there's other times you don't have to carry anything. Just a box of matches. That depends on the place you're going to do it in. It has to have strong walls. Thick. (*He moves to tap a wall*) Like these. This used to be an old farmhouse, didn't it? Not "breeze" and plaster. Good solid stuff. Yeah, this'd do fine. Then you have to have a good source of air — central — a down draught ... somewhere the oxygen can *rush* in ... (*He moves to the fireplace to bend to look up the chimney*) A straight up chimney. Lovely. But most important of all, you have to have gas.

He bends by the artificial fire and turns on the gas tap. We hear the hiss of gas. A long moment as Larry and Alex regard each other, and the only sound is the hiss of escaping gas

That gas is escaping low, and it'll stay that way, spreading across the floor like ... like an invisible carpet ... layer on layer ... building up ... thicker and thicker. In a room this size, with all the doors and windows closed, it may take three or four minutes to reach the flame of the candles. Then d'you know what's going to happen? Listen carefully, Alex, I want you to know. The gas — and there'll be a lot of gas by now, a whole lot ... it touches the flame. Instant ignition —across the whole room, and it's contained — so it explodes ... *boom*! Just like a bomb, dammit it *is* a bomb. It'll take out all the windows and maybe the doors too, but I think they'll hold. I hope so. But it doesn't matter too much. And your lungs ...? (*He slaps his hands together in a shockingly sharp sound*) It'll explode into a ball of flame. The whole room ... flame ... and then ... it'll use up the available air in one big gulp ... almost simultaneously ... more air will come down the chimney. Sucked down ... and the flame will be fed to high intensity. Everything small ... gone! This (*He touches the sofa*) a ball of fire ... even the safe will start to melt! It'll be a *furnace* in here. And you? You'll melt too, Alex. But you'll be a crisp, Alex, just a crisp ... no chair, no ties ... no you. Just a crisp ... and then ... ashes.

A pause as Alex regards him. The only sound is the hissing gas

Alex (*finally*) Jesus Christ! No! (*He begins to try and free himself, rocking the chair to and fro in his vain, desperate efforts*)

Larry It's no good, Alex. A gas leak — an accident — you know how lousy these foreign safety standards are! (*He sniffs*) That gas is building faster than I thought. I have to go now ...
Alex For pity's sake ...

Larry moves to the door

They'll get you. They'll find Suzy's body and ——
Larry No. (*He moves to open the kitchen door and pushes it wider. We can see Suzy lying inside and the blood on the walls*) That fire's going to be big enough for two. No wounds, no fractured skull. Just ashes. Two piles of ashes. Ciao, Alex. I'll light another candle for you. In Rio!

Larry quickly opens the door and exits, quickly closing the door shut behind him

Alex is alone. The gas hisses away; the candles burn. A moment and then we hear the car door slam. The car turns over but does not fire. It turns over again; this time the engine starts, and the car finally starts to move away. After a moment Suzy suddenly stirs, sits up and gets to her feet to come running from the kitchen into the main area, her body and clothes flecked with blood. Her first instinct is to release Alex

Alex The candles!

Suzy runs on to extinguish the three candles

Now the gas!

Suzy moves to turn off the gas fire

Open the doors and windows ... but careful ... don't make a spark now ...!

Suzy opens the front door, then opens the windows, then turns to move back to Alex and release him. (NB She can either untie him or use the knife to cut the bonds)

Suzy God, I thought ... when he pointed the gun at you ...

Alex He was never going to use the gun. I *told* you. (*He hurries to the phone, picks it up and dials a number*) Door.

Suzy nods, moves to the front door and starts to open and close it rapidly to make a fanning effect

Wasn't I right? (*Into the phone*) Hello? Capitan Zachares, por favor. ... Si. Alex Winder. (*To Suzy*) Didn't I tell you!? (*Into the phone*) Captain Zachares? Alex Winder. I'm up at my villa. ... Yes, yes, I'm all right ... *please just listen to me*! I just scared off an intruder ... (*listening*) No ... no ...(*He glances at Suzy*) My secretary noticed him first. Prowling around the outside — he was holding what she thought was some kind of bomb ... Obviously he thought the place was empty, yes ... but when I appeared ... he took off. In a light blue Mercedes. ... Well, he looked youngish to me ... well built ... heavily tanned. ... Yes, took off down the mountain road. ... A road block? Yes, that seems sensible. And, Captain ... Tell your men to be careful — he was carrying a gun. ... Yes, I'm quite sure. He's armed all right — and dangerous! (*He hangs up and turns to look at Suzy, then moves past her to push open the kitchen door, enters and finds a damp cloth. He starts to wipe away the blood from the walls*)

Suzy hesitates, then moves to the kitchen to help him

No, I can clean up here, you attend to yourself. The police are bound to be up here soon — clean yourself up ... and get rid of that dress.

He tosses her a wet flannel and she begins to wipe blood from her arms

Suzy I was so scared lying there. I thought any moment he would come over for a closer look.
Alex I was ready for that. If he had, I would have grabbed him, diverted him. You did fine.

Alex has just about finished wiping the walls clean by now, while Suzy pulls her bloodstained dress up over her head. She remains in her slip for a moment, then she hurries to where she has hidden a spare smock-like dress and starts to pull it on. She then moves to pick up the bloodstained dress

Suzy Ugh!

Alex (*emerging from the kitchen with the bloody cloth*) C'mon, it's only pig's blood. (*He takes the bloodstained dress from her, wraps his own cloth in it and moves to thrust them deep away in one of the desk drawers*) They won't be searching the place — no reason.

He looks to where Suzy stands frozen. He moves to take her face in his hands; she begins to shake as she starts to break up

(*Very gently*) No, not now. Not when we're at the end of the road.

Suzy Is he the man?

Alex Tell me, when you saw him that day in Altea, why did you call me? What did you expect?

Suzy You were Andy's friend. You worked on the case!

Alex And got nowhere, didn't even make an arrest.

Suzy That wasn't you, it was the people above you; "not enough hard evidence", but you ... you were always so sure it was him.

Alex And now I know.

Suzy Do you?

Alex Come on, you heard what he had in mind! A cleverly devised explosion, followed by a fire to destroy all evidence.

She stares at him and he gently moves closer to her

Andy was more than just a colleague to me, he was my friend, and I know now how horrible his death must have been ... helpless, listening to the gas hiss ... watching the candle burn ... and then ...

Suzy cries out, burying herself against him

Dutch Holland murdered your brother, you can't have any doubt about that now.

Suzy But is what we're doing any better, is it right for us to ——?

Alex (*interjecting*) It isn't legal, that's for sure, but it's justice, the kind he deserves. We've fitted him up, put him into a frame he can't escape from this time.

Suzy We're not going to get away with it!

Alex Oh, yes.

Suzy No, they'll find out, someone will find out.

Alex regards her, then moves to the phone

Alex I'll go through it again, step by step — you find one flaw, one
loophole, and I promise you I'll call Zachares and tell him to pull his
men off. Right?

Suzy nods

OK. Today he gave me that explosive device, the way we always hoped
and planned he would. But I didn't use it — instead I planted my own
homemade effort — the kind I used to blow up my car. (*He grins*) A
sacrifice, but cheap at the price. Yes, I took *my* bomb and planted it —
not in some mythical speedboat, but in the water, close to a police patrol
boat, where it exploded harmlessly, but with maximum effect. And
when I went to plant that bomb I was driving *his* car — the blue
Mercedes — and parked it where I was damned sure it was going to be
seen ... and *was* seen, I'm sure of that — I heard the excitement in
Zachares' voice when I mentioned the Mercedes ... the car he's driving
down that mountain road right now — into a waiting road block.

Suzy He's carrying a loaded gun.

Alex I warned them he's armed.

Suzy Yes, but suppose he uses it on some innocent person. We would be
responsible for ——

Alex (*interjecting*) Suzy. The gun is, and always was, loaded with blanks.
But the police don't know that, and, in the boot of the car is an explosive
device — *his* device — the one he gave me earlier today, still intact, and
still covered in his prints ... and only his. Did I forget anything?

Suzy The diamonds.

Alex Ah, yes, the diamonds. They're going to remain an enigma — what
was Dutch Holland doing with a bag full of paste stones? (*He touches
the phone*) Loopholes? Well?

Suzy (*turning away*) What will happen now?

Alex We've got two chances. One — the Spanish cops will grab him, they
are efficient, you know. They'll find out his job in Britain was bomb
maker, and conclude that he came to Spain to work for a new master.
That ... along with the evidence we've planted ...? They'll toss him in a
cell and throw away the key!

Suzy Two chances?

He looks at her

You said two chances.

Alex Ah ...(*pacing away*) These are troubled times, Suzy. Dangerous days — two bombs in this area in less than twenty-four hours? And one of them aimed at a police patrol boat? Whatever you may think, a cop is just a human being — he can get as nervous as the next man — *and trigger happy*. Particularly when he thinks he's up against an armed terrorist ...

At this moment, a long way away, we hear the rattle of gunfire, and then silence

Machine carbines. I think we got lucky.

Suzy *Lucky!*

She is close to breaking up again, but Alex moves to grip her

Alex Don't think of *him*, think of Andy. There would have been one, brief moment — as he felt his lungs collapse, and then smelt his own flesh as he began to fry! *Think of Andy!*

Suzy What we've done is outside the law.

Alex The law? *I'm* the law — Detective Inspector Alex Winder ... and I could do nothing — until now. The law's an impotent ass — we did what it couldn't. We trapped and twisted and turned him, and led him ——

Suzy (*interjecting*) Like a lamb to the slaughter.

Alex Not a lamb, Suzy. Not a lamb. A ruthless, bloody murderer!

They stare at each other and then the phone rings. Alex picks it up

Yes?... Yes, Captain ... what! How the hell ...? No, wait a minute ... wait ...

The line goes dead, he rattles the receiver, then turns to regard Suzy

Larry got away.

Suzy What!?

Alex They shot at him, but he got away.

A pause as this sinks in. During this we hear a car approaching, and a beat or so later Alex and Suzy become aware of the sound. The car is coming up fast

Suzy It's him. Oh, my God!

The car comes to a stop, the engine dies, and we hear a door slam. Then silence. Alex moves at last — to snatch up the fire iron — and turn towards the door with it just as the door slams open

> *Larry enters and stands there, regarding them. He is very still and erect, and he holds the explosive device. The only sound is its ticking*

Larry Set up! I knew it, I was ... set up ...!

He moves now, coming further into the room — Alex steps back, holding the fire iron as a weapon — but then Larry tosses the device forward into the room, takes another step, and falls forward. We see that his back is a mass of blood. He lies, his outstretched hand just touching the device

Alex tosses the fire iron down, quickly moves to Larry and the device, and as he does so, pulls out a handkerchief and uses it to finally switch off the ticking of the device. This done, he expertly feels Larry's neck for a pulse. There is none, and finally he straightens up to look at Suzy

Alex A kind of justice.

They regard each other, standing to either side of Larry's body. Far off, we hear a police siren approaching

CURTAIN

FURNITURE AND PROPERTY LIST

ACT I

Scene 1

On stage: Desk with chair. *In it/on it:* telephone, telephone pad, papers, matches, ashtray, knife, box of ammunition and explosive device
Sofa
Mirror
Toledo steel daggers
Three-pronged candelabra
Artificial log gas fire
Set of fire irons
Small table
Drinks tray
Transistor radio
Large oil painting on hinges *Behind it:* wall safe containing gun, papers, and suede bag of diamonds

Personal: **Larry:** gold watch

Scene 2

On stage: As before

Off stage: Torch — practical **(Larry)**

Personal: **Larry:** dark jacket, surgical gloves

Scene 3

On stage: As before

Off stage: Cardboard box of alcohol bottles (**Alex**)

Personal: **Alex**: car keys, pack of cigars

ACT II

SCENE 1

Set: Broken panes of leaded glass

SCENE 2

Strike: Broken glass

Off stage: Valise containing explosive device (**Larry**)

Personal: **Larry**: car keys
              Alex: handkerchief

SCENE 3

Set: Half-full whisky bottle and valise on desk
        Damp cloths and blood on walls in kitchen
        Smock-like dress

Off stage   Nil

Personal: **Suzy**: apron
              Alex: handkerchief

LIGHTING PLOT

Property fittings required: interior lighting
Practical fittings required: desk lamp

ACT I, SCENE 1   Afternoon

To open: General effect of daylight

No cues

ACT I, SCENE 2   Night

To open: General effect of night

Cue 1   **Alex** moves to switch on main lights   (Page 10)
            Snap on interior lighting

ACT I, SCENE 3   Morning

To open: General effect of morning light

Cue 2   **Larry:** "OK, I'll ..."   (Page 28)
            Flash through windows from explosion

ACT II, SCENE 1   Early afternoon

To open: General effect of daylight

No cues

ACT II, SCENE 2   Late afternoon

To open: General effect of late afternoon light

No cues

ACT II, SCENE 3   Night

To open: General effect of night

No cues

EFFECTS PLOT

ACT I

ACT II

PRINTED IN GREAT BRITAIN BY
THE LONGDUNN PRESS LTD BRISTOL
MADE IN ENGLAND